Jan 9, 1990

To a lovely lady

Mary Louise Jones

Woody Watches the Masters

WOODY WATCHES THE MASTERS:

Book I:
Four Great Artists

Mary Louise Jordan Jones

VANTAGE PRESS
New York / Washington / Atlanta
Los Angeles / Chicago

Illustrated by Eideen Molloy

FIRST EDITION

All rights reserved, including the right of
reproduction in whole or in part in any form.

Copyright © 1984 by Mary Louise Jordan Jones

Published by Vantage Press, Inc.
516 West 34th Street, New York, New York 10001

Manufactured in the United States of America
ISBN: 533-05814-7

To Ima Jackson Jordan, Ella Jordan Knuth,
and Daphine Reed Jordan

Contents

Foreword ix
Meet Woody the Bookworm xi

Michelangelo
  Michelangelo and the Sistine Chapel 3
  Michelangelo Buonarroti 6
  Woody and Michelangelo 8
  Michelangelo 10
da Vinci
  Leonardo da Vinci and the *Mona Lisa* 13
  Leonardo da Vinci 14
  Woody Watches Leonardo da Vinci 15
  Leonardo da Vinci 19
Rembrandt
  Rembrandt and the *Night Watch* 23
  Rembrandt van Rijn 24
  Rembrandt van Rijn (*Song*) 26
Raphael
  Raphael Sanzio, the Charmer 31
  Raphael 33
  Raphael Sanzio 35
  Woody's Farewell until Book II 36

Foreword

Woody the bookworm is a lovable character who slips into the studios and workplaces of four Renaissance period artists in Italy and Holland and tells children about what he sees and hears in poetry and song. The book is designed for the first grader, but can be understood by much younger children. They will love Woody. Older children can read about Woody themselves.

Meet Woody the Bookworm

Woody was a bookworm.
Woodrow was his name,
A very dignified name,
But everyone called him "Woody"
Just the same.

Because he loved his book-home
And the friends he met inside,
He soon knew every artist,
Although he had to hide.

About the artists of the Renaissance
Woody had gleefully read,
So out from the book he crawled,
Knowing there was excitement ahead.

Because he was nearsighted
And he wanted to see more,
Perched upon his little nose,
Were the glasses that he wore.

And on his head for all to see
Was a jaunty, gay beret,
With powers that were magical,
To help him find his way.

Seeing the Sistine Chapel,
He tossed up his beret.
He had reached his journey's ending,
So he shouted out, "Hooray!"

"Go with me," says Woody,
"On an adventure bright and gay.
Go with me to Italy and Holland,
Back to the Renaissance for a stay."

Michelangelo

Michelangelo and the Sistine Chapel

Woody found himself in Rome.
He was in the Sistine Chapel.
He crawled from the book.
He heard scraping from above.

Woody turned his eyes upward.
He could see the ceiling a little better.
Near the ceiling was Michelangelo Buonarroti (Bone-na-rowti).
He was on his back on a platform. (The platform is called a scaffold.)

Michelangelo was painting a fresco on the ceiling.
A fresco is a painting done with wet plaster.
Michelangelo took the story for his painting from the Bible.
He used many figures.
His figures told the story of the Book of Genesis.

It began with the Creation of the world.
It ended with the Flood.
Michelangelo showed the dividing of the light from the darkness.
He also showed the Creation of the sun, stars, and water.

Near the center of the fresco, he showed God.
God was creating Adam.
From this, the painting gets its name.
It is called the *Creation of Adam*.

Woody studied the painting.
The painting was almost finished.
Michelangelo had worked alone.
The task had taken about four years.

The Sistine Chapel is in the Vatican, in Rome, Italy.
I hope that you can visit there and see it someday.
Woody would be pleased if you could.

Michelangelo Buonarroti

Born in Italy,
His hours were filled.
He was happy to carve
And happy to build.

On the Sistine ceiling
He painted his pride,
To show the creation of man,
With God at his side.

Woody and Michelangelo

Woody crawled from the book in the artist's studio
So that he could watch the artist at work.
Each day Woody had hidden behind blocks of stone
And watched.

The artist was Michelangelo Buonarroti (Bone-na-rowti).
Michelangelo lived and worked in Italy.
That is where the great Renaissance began.
Renaissance means "rebirth"—rebirth of learning.

Michelangelo was a sculptor.
He was also a painter and a builder.
He excelled in all.

One day Michelangelo found a very large piece of marble.
Woody watched.
Michelangelo began to chip away at the stone.

Woody had to be very careful.
The stone chips flew in every direction.

Finally the piece of sculpture was finished.

Michelangelo had carved *David*.
Woody had read in the Bible about David.
So he knew that David killed the giant Goliath.

Woody liked Michelangelo's *David*.
You will like it, too
When you see it someday
In the Academy in Florence, Italy.

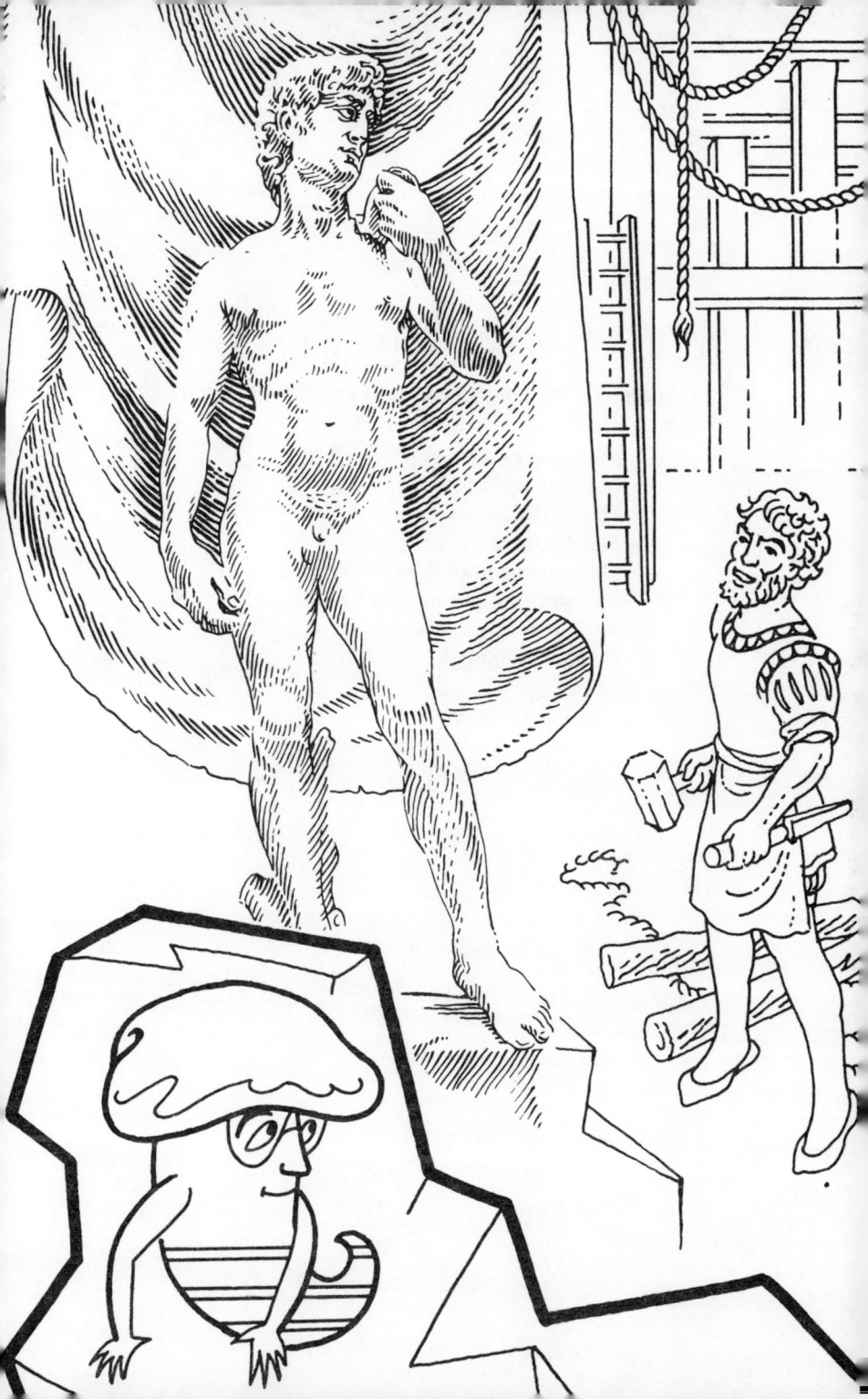

Michelangelo

(Song—To be sung to the tune of "Three Blind Mice")

Michelangelo
Michelangelo
Happy to build,
Happy to carve.
He painted Man created by God.
He carved in stone and he planned a dome.
All his life he worked with all his might
Did Michelangelo!

da Vinci

Leonardo da Vinci and the *Mona Lisa*

One day Woody was in a different studio.
The studio belonged to Leonardo da Vinci (vin-chee).

Soon Woody heard people talking.
They had come to visit Leonardo.
Woody quickly ran to a hiding place.
There he could hear the people and Leonardo.

They were asking Leonardo about a painting.
Woody knew which one they meant.
Woody had watched Leonardo paint the lady with the beautiful smile.
He, too, loved the painting of the beautiful lady.

Woody heard Leonardo tell the people that the painting was not finished.
Yet it looked finished to them.
They wanted to take it.
Leonardo would not part with it.

Woody did not know that the painting would never leave the artist until his death.
Could it be that the artist had fallen in love with his masterpiece— or possibly his model!

The *Mona Lisa* is sometimes called "La Gioconda." (Rhymes with La jee-a-conda.)
The small painting was once shown in America.
The *Mona Lisa* hangs in the Louvre (rhymes with move).
The Louvre is a museum in Paris, France.

You can look forward to seeing it there one day.
Woody would want you to see it.

Leonardo da Vinci

Leonardo wrote from right to left,
And sometimes upside down.
Lefthanded, backward, he wrote,
About things that he found.

Nature he loved and drew,
Records in journals tell
Not only the shapes of things
But the how and why as well.

Woody Watches Leonardo da Vinci

It was early in the day
But Woody was sleepy.
He crawled out of his home, a book,
And rubbed his eyes.

Woody stretched out on the table and fell asleep.
He was awakened by the sound of ladders scraping across the floor.
Near Woody were buckets of plaster, trowels, and paint.
Woody immediately knew that the bearded artist was Leonardo da Vinci.

Leonardo was working on the end wall of the large room.
Woody rubbed his eyes again.
He saw on the wall an almost-completed painting.
The painting was *The Last Supper.*

The painting was a fresco.
A fresco is a painting done with paint and wet plaster.
In the painting Jesus was seated in the center.
His disciples were seated on each side of Him.

Leonardo designed his painting well.
All lines lead the viewer's eye to Christ.
Christ was speaking to His disciples.
He told them that one of them would betray Him.

Leonardo lived over four hundred years ago.
He lived at the same time as Michelangelo.
They both lived in Italy.
They were both great during their lifetime.

Little did Leonardo know that his painting would even have
    a door built into it.
Little did he know that his fresco would withstand the bombing
    of World War II.
The three other walls of the building fell.
The wall with the painting was protected by sandbags.

After World War II, the building was restored.
The beautiful fresco was cleaned, inch by inch.
You can view the painting today.
It is in St. Mary of Grace Church in Milan, Italy.
It would please Woody if you could.

Leonardo da Vinci

(Song—To be sung to the tune of "Old MacDonald Had a Farm")

Leonardo da Vinci was an Italian man
E-I-E-I-O
And in his studio he drew a plan
E-I-E-I-O
With a painting here
And a sculpture there
   Sketches
   Sketches
Everywhere sketches.

Leonardo da Vinci was an Italian man
E-I-E-I-O
And the first airplane he did plan
E-I-E-I-O
With a parachute here
And a drawbridge there
   Parachutes
   Parachutes
Everywhere parachutes.

Leonardo da Vinci was an Italian man
E-I-E-I-O
His *Last Supper* he did plan
E-I-E-I-O
With a painting here
And a painting there
   Paintings
   Paintings
Everywhere paintings.

Leonardo da Vinci was an Italian man
    E-I-E-I-O
The *Mona Lisa* he did paint
    E-I-E-I-O
With a beautiful smile here
And a beautiful smile there
    Smiling
    Smiling
Everywhere smiling.

Leonardo da Vinci was an Italian man
And a very great man was he.

Rembrandt

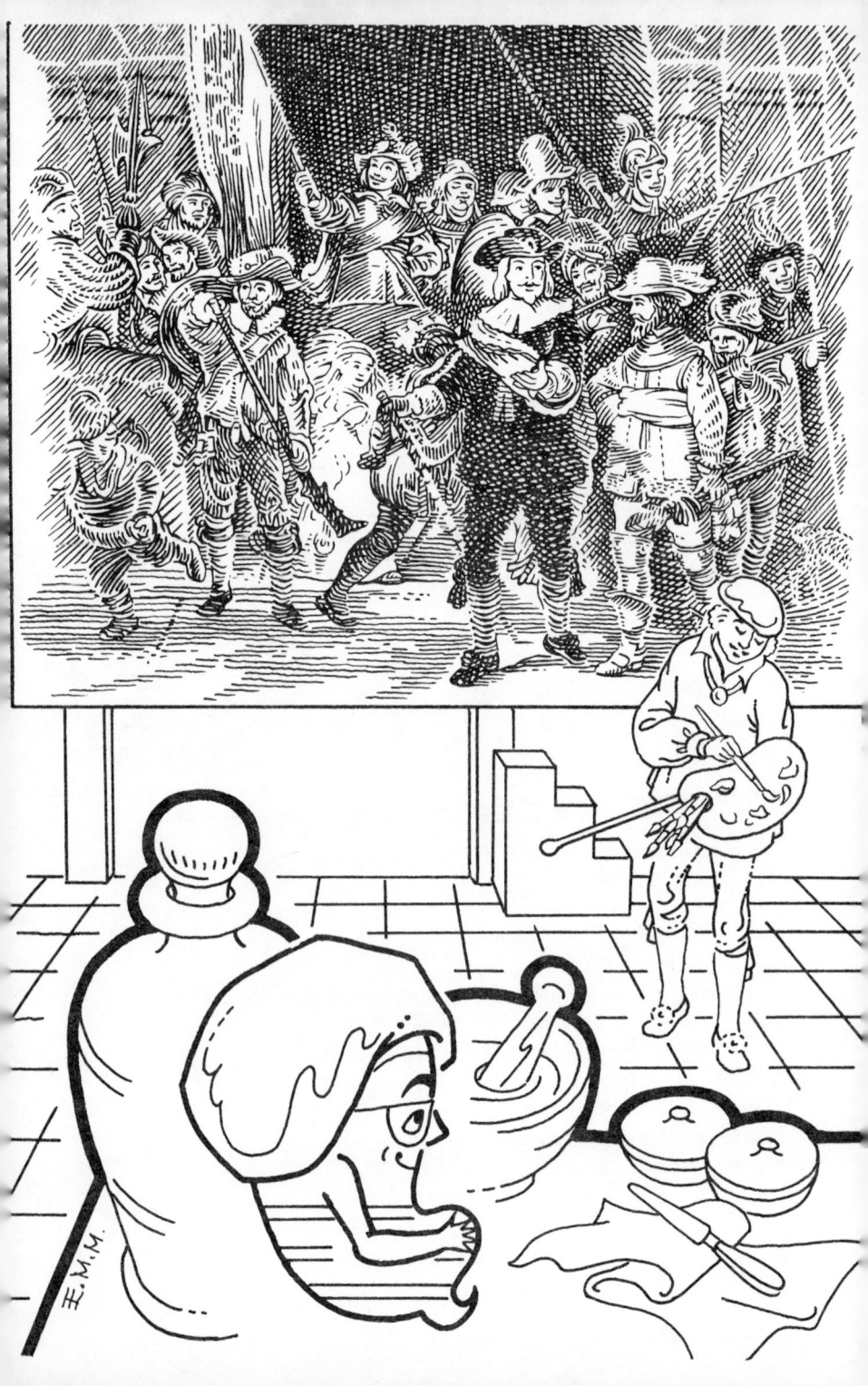

Rembrandt and the *Night Watch*

One morning Woody crawled over
To watch the great Dutch painter.
The painter was Rembrandt van Rijn (rhymes with line).
He lived about four hundred years ago.
He lived in Holland.

Rembrandt was mixing his paints.
He was working on a very large canvas.
Woody hid behind pots of paint.
He quietly watched.

Rembrandt had first placed his drawing on the canvas.
He then mixed his colors with oil.

Rembrandt began to paint with a warm golden brown.
He painted the brown around groups of people.

The members of the Civic Guard had hired him.
They wanted him to portray them to the world.

Rembrandt took his brushes that were loaded with paint.
With the masterful strokes of genius,
He arranged people into groups.
He even included a young girl.

Woody watched with interest.
The great master of light and shade developed the painting.
Woody crawled back into the book.
Each day he reappeared to watch the master painter.

Finally the painting was completed.
Rembrandt stood back and studied it with approval.
Woody heard a knock at the door.
He crawled back behind the pots of paint.

The men of the Civic Guard came to see their painting.
They expected to see themselves as a group of important men.
The men were very displeased.
They asked the artist to make changes in the painting.

Rembrandt liked the painting.
He refused to change it.
The men did not accept or pay for the painting.

Rembrandt was pleased to keep the masterpiece.
However, because of it, he lost popularity.
He lived to be quite old, but was penniless.
Today the *Night Watch* is the most famous painting in the Rijks
    (rhymes with dikes)
Museum in Amsterdam, Holland.
People from all over the world go to view it.
Someday you may, too. That would please Woody very much.

Rembrandt van Rijn

To Rembrandt a great love
Was Saskia, his wife,
She posed for his work,
She gave strength to his life.

Saskia he painted
In dress and in bath,
The crown of his glory,
The love of his life.

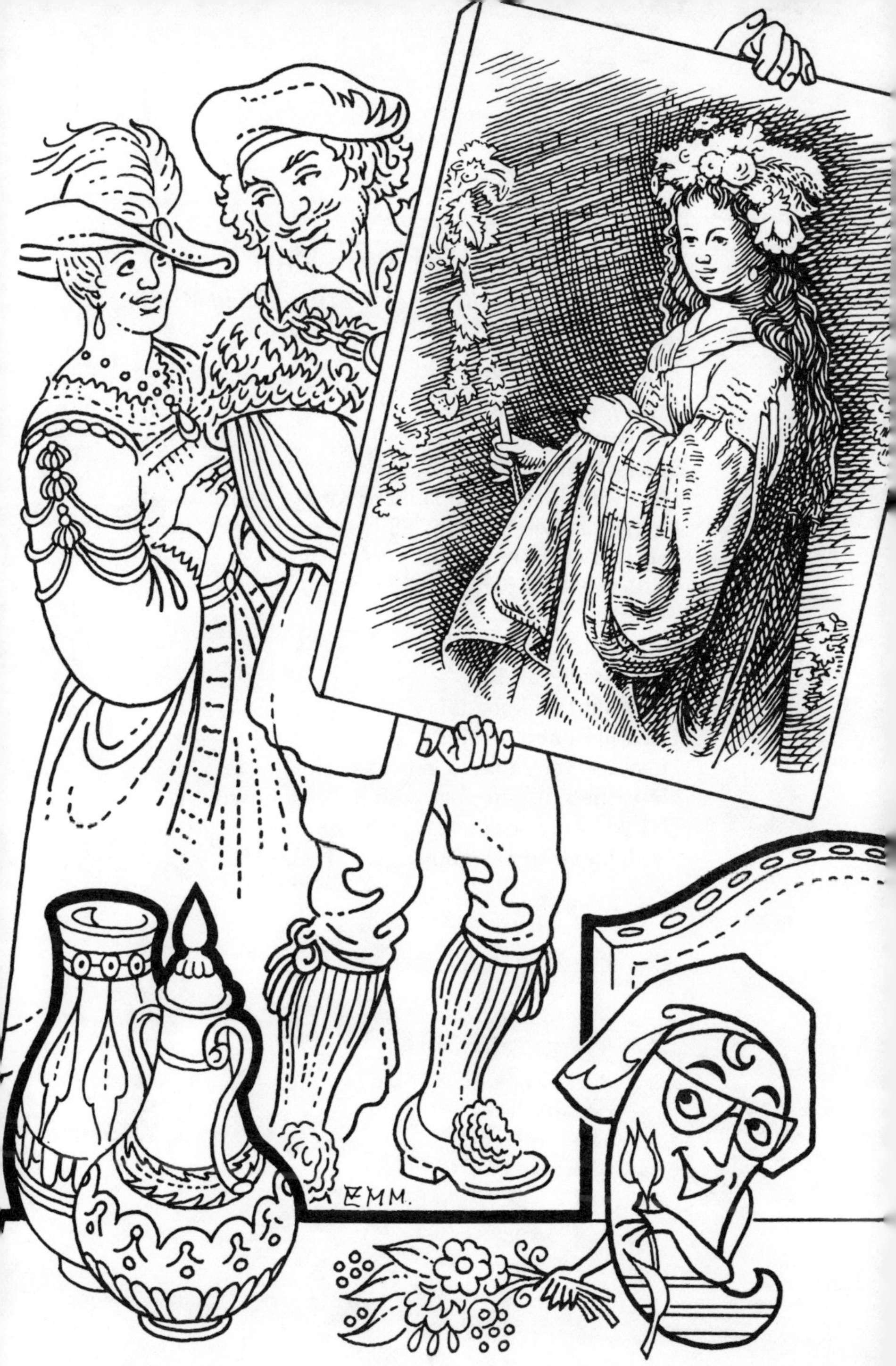

Rembrandt van Rijn
(Song—To be sung to the tune of "Three Blind Mice")

Rembrandt van Rijn
Rembrandt van Rijn
See how he paints!
See how he paints!
He always painted in somber tones,
He had a style that was all his own.
Did you ever see such a pure delight
As Rembrandt van Rijn!

Rembrandt van Rijn
Rembrandt van Rijn
Used light and shade!
Used light and shade!
He chose the Bible to get his theme,
He bathed his subjects with light from within,
Did you ever see such a sight sublime
As Rembrandt van Rijn.

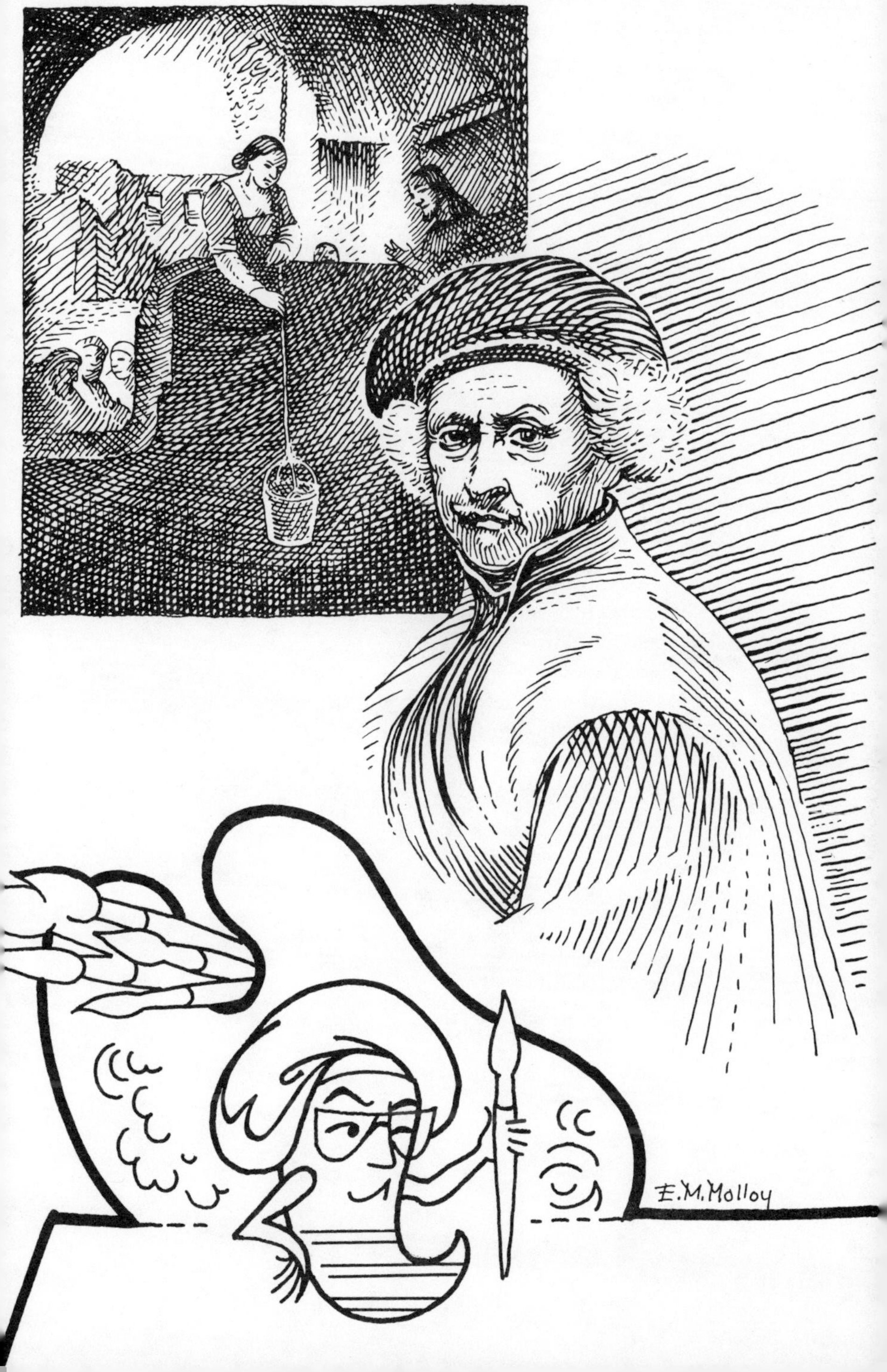
E.M.Molloy

Raphael

Raphael Sanzio, the Charmer

Woody knew about Raphael.
He knew that Raphael was born in Italy.
Woody knew that Raphael lived during the Renaissance, over four hundred years ago.

Woody was impressed with the fine painting that Raphael did.
Raphael began painting while still a young man.
He was skilled in giving individuality to each person he painted.

Raphael's charm, sweetness and appearance well suited the nobility.
They invited him to paint for them.
The Church also bid for his services.
He won favor with all of them.

Woody watched Raphael as he painted religious subjects.
Raphael painted the Baby Jesus and His Mother.
Such a painting is called the *Madonna and Child.*
Woody especially liked these paintings.

At the height of Raphael's fame and fortune
He was struck down by fever.
At the age of thirty-seven, he died.
Do you not wonder what he could have done had he lived longer? Woody wonders, too.

Raphael's *Sistine Madonna* hangs today in the museum in Dresden, East Germany.

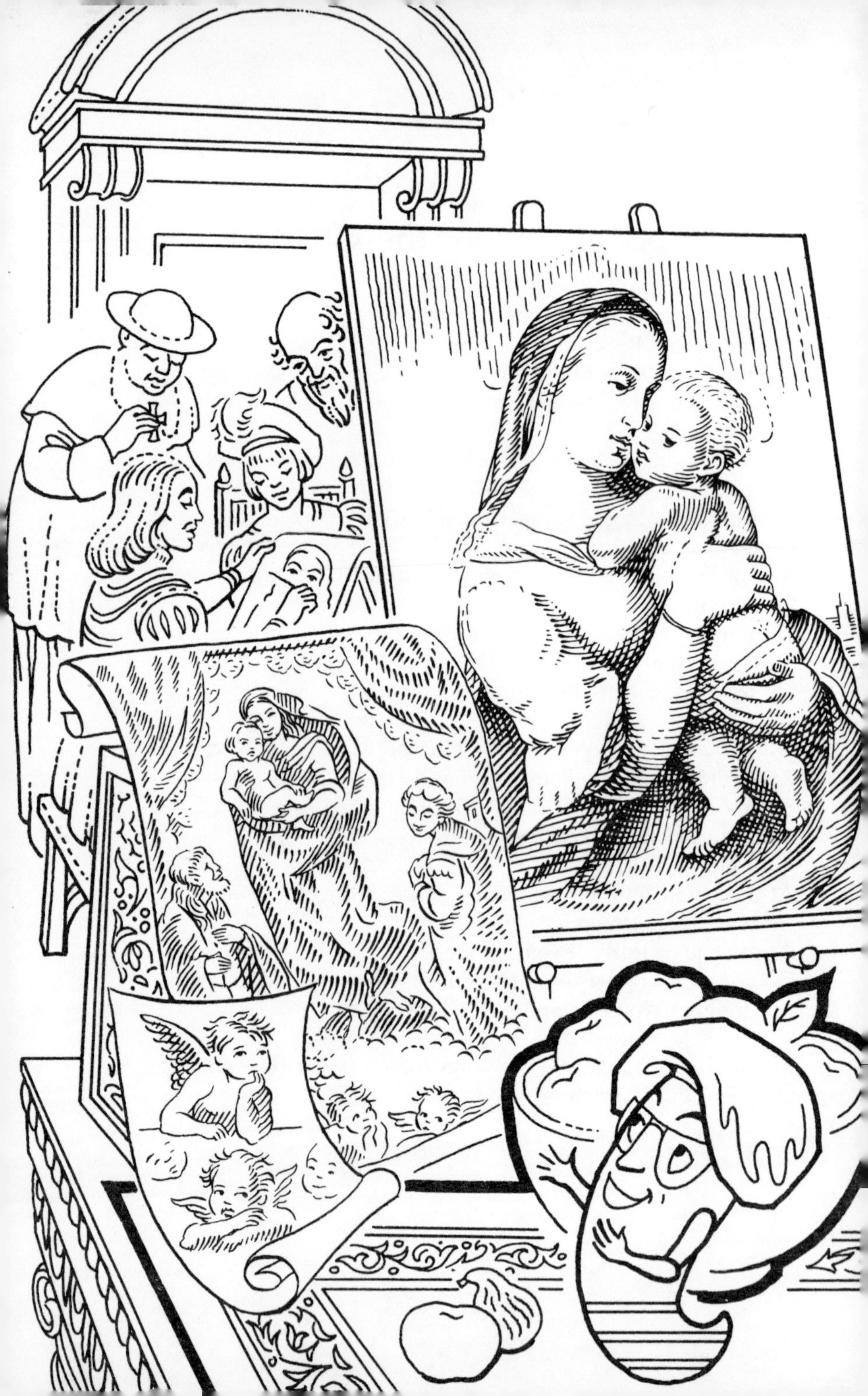

Raphael

(Song—To be sung to the tune of "Row, Row, Row Your Boat")

Raph, Raph, Raphael
Gently did he paint,
Madonnas, Madonnas,
Madonnas, Madonnas,
And then he did a saint.

Raph, Raph, Raphael
Charming he was, and young;
Dashing, Dashing,
Dashing, Dashing,
Pleasing all the throng.

Raph, Raph, Raphael
Great and kind of heart,
Friends, Friends,
Friends, Friends,
In Italy and other parts.

Raph, Raph, Raphael
Died quite young, they say.
Fever, Fever,
Fever, Fever,
Took the master away.

Raph, Raph, Raphael
Left his print on time,
Glorious, Glorious,
Glorious, Glorious,
Were his works so fine.

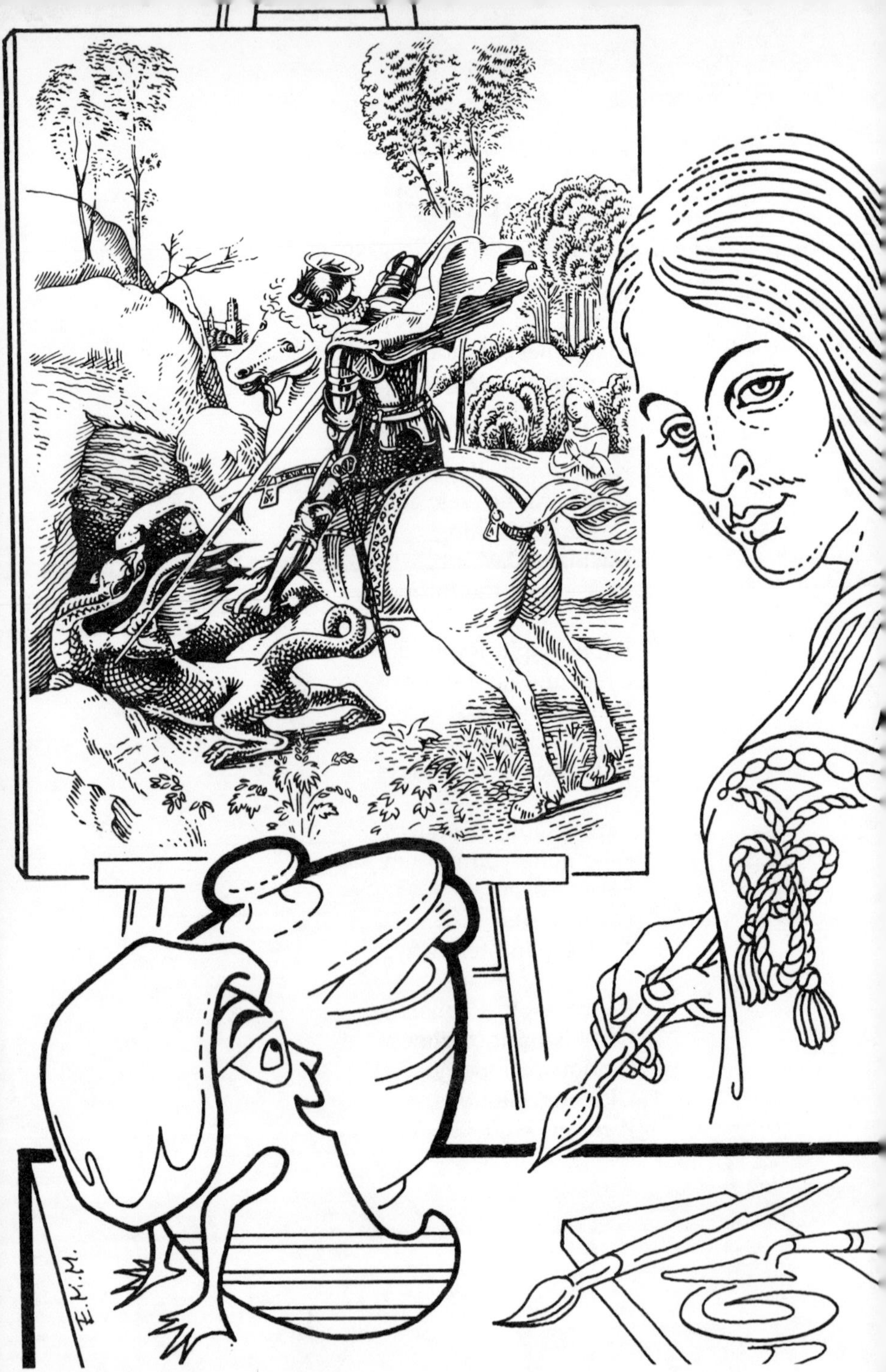
E.M.M.

Raphael Sanzio

Liked by Michelangelo,
And a foe of none.
Raphael was loved
For himself alone.

The fact that he did well
In all things that he tried,
Brought Church and State
Both to his side.

Young, dapper and bright,
He painted and drew,
Throughout his short life
To bring pleasure to you.

Woody's Farewell until Book II

"Bye for now," says Woody.
"It was fun to show you around.
In Book II to France we'll go
To see painters of world renown."